Dispatches from the Dnipro

Dispatches from the Dnipro

Poems on the War in Ukraine

KYLE JANKOWSKI

FOREWORD BY CLIFFORD MAYES

Dispatches from the Dnipro: Poems on the War in Ukraine by Kyle Jankowski

Copyright © 2023 Kyle Jankowski, Siubhail Publishing, LLC

First hardcover printing, 2023. Second Printing 2024
First softcover printing, 2024.

ISBN: 979-8-9900005-1-3

First English Edition: December 2023

Cover Art: *Reply of the Zaporozhian Cossacks to the Sultan of Turkey* by Ilya Repin (1893), Ukrainian/Russian painter. (Ukrainian) Запорожці пишуть листа турецькому султанові (1893). (Polish) "Kozacy piszą list do sułtana" (druga niedokończona wersja z 1893 r.), Ilja Riepin. (Hebrew) 1893 תשובת הקוזאקים הזפורוז'יים לסולטאן תורכיה מאת איליה רפין. Use of this painting is in the public domain.

Siubhail Publishing, LLC, USA
www.siubhailpublishingllc.com

via Amazon Kindle Direct Publishing

AUTHOR'S NOTE ON
THE COVER ART
Reply of the Zaporozhian Cossacks to the Sultan of Turkey
by Ilya Repin (1893)

This painting is known by other names such as *Cossacks of Saporog Are Drafting a Manifesto*, and *Cossacks are Writing a Letter to the Turkish Sultan*. The historical scene depicted is of Ukrainian Cossacks drafting a taunting, insulting and vulgar letter, eventually sent to Sultan Mehmed IV. Mehmed, leader of the invading Ottoman Empire had demanded the people of the Ukraine submit to Ottoman (Islamic) Rule, despite the Sultan's armies having suffered significant defeat in battles with the Ukrainians. Centuries later, another famous reply letter was sent from the American Army liberators at Bastogne, France (December 1944) in response to the German Commander's letter, which had requested the Americans surrender. The American commander's reply was only one word, "Nuts!"

The painting is interpreted as demonstrating the absurdity of the request, and the Ukrainians' great pleasure at drafting a satirical and progressively absurd response letter to the Sultan's even more ridiculous demands of surrender and submission to his rule. I felt this famous Ukrainian art was a fitting analogy for the current situation in Ukraine, whereas Russia's leadership is justifying their war, in part, by a Russian sentiment of eminent domain over Ukraine's sovereignty, land, government, industries, economy, ports, and even children.

CHARITIABLE DONATION DISCLOSURE

A percentage of the annual profit of the sales of the combined print and e-book versions will be donated to a registered and accredited charity serving Ukrainian refugees, the rebuilding of Ukraine, or other related humanitarian services. No proceeds will be used to purchase military hardware or weapons.

MORE BOOKS BY
KYLE JANKOWSKI

"The Poet as Archetypal Teacher in Unteachable Times"
in
New Visions and New Voices: Extending the Principles of Archetypal Psychology to Include a Variety of Venues, Issues, and Projects (Vol. 2)
-(Eds.) Clifford Mayes & Jacquelyn Ann Rinaldi
In print Spring 2023, Roman & Littlefield Publishers

Unorthodox: Poems on Christmas, Hanukkah and Winter
Part 1 of the Liturgy Trilogy
In print Christmas 2024, Siubhail Publishing, LLC

The Mermaid and Her Sword:
New Polish Proverbs for Perilous Times
In print Spring 2025, Siubhail Publishing, LLC

For more information on upcoming projects, release dates, poetry readings, please visit www.siubhailpublishingllc.com.

To Our Lady of Perpetual Help

Acknowledgments

Vanessa, Susie, Danuta, Ukrainian journalists, Ukrainian friends, Norman Davies, and many others which space prevents me from mentioning, but whose work was profound. Any errors in this book are entirely my responsibility.

TABLE OF CONTENTS

Foreword
  Clifford Mayes   17

Introduction
  Kyle Jankowski   33

War Letters
  War Letters   37
  What the Firebird Knew   38
  The Enemy is Us   39
  My Palindrome Birthday   40
  Material Advantage   41
  Homeland   42

Vita, Dulcedo, et Spes Nostra, Salve
(Our life, our sweetness, and our hope, save us.)
  Nesting Doll Psychology   45
  Theotokos   46
  Eikon   48
  Straightening Tool   49
  Ink on the Wind   50
  Thinking About Journalism in Russia   51
  War Marriages   52
  A Polish Poet Praises Ukrainian Women   53

Cossacks and Polacks
  A Polonia Speaks to Ukrainians About Betrayal   57
  Half Blind   59
  For Your Freedom and Ours   61
  Growing Freedom   63
  Slavic Brethren   64
  The Falcons are Returning to Ukraine   66
  Si vis pacem, para bellum   67
  Slav Incognito   69
  The Blue and the Gold   71
  Ode to the Daughters of Ukraine   73
  Tribute to Ukraine's Theater Troupes   74

Odes to the New Firebird

Graffiti on a Wall of a Collapsed Ukrainian School   77
Brief to an Aspiring Tyrant   78
Russian Grey   80
Modern Warfare   81
Koan for the Disappeared   83
The Wastelands Tyrants Create   84
Dispatch from the Dnipro   86
Historical Notes on the Russia-Ukraine War   87
Russian Roulette   89
Shashlik   90
Russian Soldier's Wives   91
Wag the Dog   92

After the Guns Go Silent

After the Guns Go Silent   95
Resurrection of Ukraine   97
In Sunflower Fields   98
The Easter Sun Rises   99

Author's Bio

101

Reader's Notes

103

FOREWORD

By Clifford Mayes

"The test of a first-rate intelligence is the ability to hold
two opposed ideas in the mind at the same time,
and still retain the ability to function."
-F. Scott Fitzgerald

The Poet and the Transcendent Function

One of the most important influences on Kyle Jankowski as both a psychotherapist and a poet is the work of the Swiss psychiatrist Carl Jung. Jung is best known for his idea of the archetypes and the collective unconscious. But perhaps even more key to Jungian psychology is his lesser-known notion of "the transcendent function" (Miller, 2004). Because this concept is, I believe, crucial to know in reading this important young poet, it merits a bit of unpacking. This "function" (or psychospiritual process) is called "transcendent" because it refers to how, optimally, the psyche, when confronted with the seemingly irreconcilable opposites which life relentlessly throws at us, has the capacity to attain a "transcendent" (or more evolved) vision that not only includes the best of those opposites but also goes beyond them.

This resolution of a polarity typically takes the shape of a symbol because the semantic and emotional multivalence of a symbol allows it to not only contain but also transcend the apparent contradiction that was straining the language of either side, causing these apparently antithetical discourses to dissolve into shrill invectives against each other. This new symbol is the foundation and origin of a new language, a new worldview, a higher plane of discourse more complex, and therefore more productive.

Engaging in this dialectical process in productively dealing with life's constant conundrums is what Jung called the individuation process, which really just boils down to becoming more nuanced and mature in response to life's intractable complexity. As such, individuation is not a once-in-a-lifetime affair. Beginning somewhere around midlife, according to Jung, individuation requires ongoing practice and honing throughout all of the second phase of life up until one's death. It is not that all conflicts get erased. They don't—although some might. The problems may even repeat themselves from time to time. Thus, one should look at individuation as an upward spiral, recursively encountering the same dilemmas from time to time but doing so at higher and higher levels.

Jankowski aims in this volume at stimulating this process in the reader—here on the unlikely stage of the killing fields of Ukraine—since this world-historical event is so key to Jankowski's own individuation processes as a Pole who has deeply feels his Slavic roots from the beginning in his Polish-American, rust-belt, blue-collar birth place and first home in Flint, Michigan.

Indeed, here is the first paradox in Jankowski's poetry. On one hand, he is a patriot whose love of America, tempered in his immediate and extended family's auto-workers' and skilled-trades ethos, is as solid and true as a brand-new 1960 Chevy that just rolled proudly off the conveyor belt in America's heyday to capture a booming national market while Dinah Shore sang, "See the USA in a Chevrolet. America's the greatest land of all" on television that night. *These colors don't run!* And yet, there is no cultural analyst more aware of America's historical and present shortcomings, even crimes, than Kyle Jankowski, or more trenchant in his critique. He has the heart of a Marine Drill Sergeant and the social conscience of a university sociologist.

Each night after a full day's work as a psychotherapist,
Fending off the sting and tedium of the thousand paper cuts that
       the fashionably neurotic American
Inflicts upon himself and me,
(The one-thousand concentrated cuts along the artery of my throat)
With the Dollar Store paper of their "dysfunctions"—
As if the soul were just a faulty machine to align
To official specs

Or of refusing to be a projection screen for their glib atheism
Or embarrassing reboots of Sixties drug fantasies,
And after exorcising the screaming wraiths that come
Streaming out of their existential quagmires,

I finally return home,
Landing at my campaign desk.

The votive lit,
A chaplet counted,
I sit in silence.

And yet, side by side with his often-caustic critiques of postmodern America—its moral absences and self-indulgent excesses— are outpourings of love and gratitude for what it means to him as ethnically a Slav and ecclesiastically a Roman Catholic to have been born in a land that shelters those who would otherwise be living in the specter of one atheistic, racist bully or another and their armies of horror on either the Right or Left.

Hence, the juxtaposition of, first, his abundant life as a native-born American who has a successful practice as a psychotherapist in and around Chicago with, second, his terror-drenched, decimated Slavic brothers and sisters in Ukraine, who labor under the specter of the vicious and voracious former KGB agent and current president of Russia, Vladimir Putin—or, if not him, some other world-historical villain. In "Blue and Gold," Jankowski juxtaposes the plight of his Ukrainian cousins with his life of safety and abundance.

On this unusually crisp Palm Sunday, I set out into the
    wilderness.
Tying two bandannas around my greyhound's naked neck,
    one royal blue, one gold,
I think of Ukraine's still cool hued skies and frosted and
    faded flaxen fields.

The blue and the gold were woven into my fate long before
    my birth—
The Polish *Jastrzębiec* Clan,
    to which I owe half my ancient heraldry.
The coat of arms of the ancient Jankowski family line,
    one of the first families knighted and bestowed the
        title *Szlachta,*
    for chivalric service and sacrifice to the young
        burgeoning Polish Kingdom.
My *alma mater,* The University of Michigan,
    arena gridiron tournaments where sport stands in
        for warfare,
    the source of this simple blue kerchief now adorning
        my loyal hound.

Later that week, conditioning for the annual Chicago Polish
    Marian Pilgrimage
    (the source of the gold scarf)
I traverse tarnished but reclaimed Midwestern prairies,
Long cold, now thawing, brightening, gradually enlivening,
With Spring songbirds and blooming birches.

Painfully, I envisage my Ukrainian friends living among
    missile cratered golden grain fields.

Jankowski, the (Truly) Counter-Cultural Poet

The concept of the transcendent function helps us make sense of the truly counter-cultural quality of the poetry contained in this volume. For, on one hand, Jankowski will not, as is today the fashion in our fractious society, cling to anything simplistic or programmatic on either the ideological Left or Right, for that would be to ignore the dialectical complexity of things. But on the other hand, neither will this poet allow the reader to wander off into an ethical relativism because of that complexity. Rather, Jankowski suggests, indeed even insists, that his readers—each in his or her own fashion—define and refine their own ethical perspectives; for, there is no individuation in the individual if he or she lacks an ethical core, and there is no democracy without such individuals in creative and civil debate with each other.

Jankowski reveals his own core commitments in this volume, but never to dogmatically insist upon them but rather to model what it means to *have* such commitments in the first place—another supremely countercultural move by Jankowski at a time when ethical commitments in all their existential complexity are increasingly being supplanted by political assertions in all their self-serving oversimplification. This makes of Jankowski not only a counter-cultural poet but also a highly intelligent one if we take on board F. Scott Fitzgerald's definition of intelligence as "the ability to hold two contradictory ideas together in one's mind at the same time, yet go on functioning"—a good working example of the phenomenological plight of the individual under the traitorous sway of genius. It is also makes of him a highly topical poet but one whose savvy about the present is profoundly tempered by his study of the past.

Jankowski's central commitment is as a Catholic. Yet although devout, he is no cut-and-dried, strictly-by-the-book member of a church. He could hardly be that and still carry on his practice as a psychotherapist treating a wide range of "dysfunctions"—or "illnesses" as he would more frankly put it to avoid the mechanistic, medically-modelled view of the human being as merely a soft machine with technical problems—"disorders" or "dysfunctions". Nor would his vocation as a poet be possible if he always stuck to official scripts of any institution. In this regard as well as in others, Jankowski's poetry evidences the most curious blend of an almost medieval chivalric delicacy and a 21st-Century Chicagoan's urban irony.

We see this in the poem "Growing Freedom," where Jankowski does the almost unthinkable in the current political environment by juxtaposing a dire, dour "Berkeley feminist" making yet another dreadful political point, on one hand, with the much more animating ways and charms of the traditional Ukrainian woman, on the other.

> In Ukraine,
> Mothers and fathers still remember they are the future's
>   caretakers.
> Each day, after dressing and feeding the children, they then
>   dedicate themselves
> To their lifelong work:
> Resurrecting a starved, exiled and slaughtered culture
>   (the soul of the nation).
>
> In this way, they are more animating than any Berkeley
>   feminist.
>
>> Deftly, they embroider contemporary *vyshyvka* on new
>> Levi's and rustic wedding vests.

With untethered tongues, they tell the story of their almost
    forgotten ancestry.
With hands ever ancient ever new, they spin out the links
    and mend the tears, on the tapestry of
Ukraine's cultural loom.

In this way, they are more avant-garde than the latte-laden
    scene in California and New York.

Similarly, in "Ode to Ukrainian Women," Jankowski offers us
verbal sketches of:

Ukrainian *women*—
Comfortable oiling Kalashnikovs and iron skillets.
Equally clever with navigating home economics, Soviet
    Five-Year-Plans and selling their elegant paintings
    through internet commerce.
Adept at scientific matters, I.T. centers, translating Cyrillic
    and Latin letters.
Unashamedly proficient at soothing children, animals, and
    mental patients.
Experts in laundry room, boardroom and bedroom.
Adroitly dancing across battlefields with *Shashka*, or manor
    house with *szlachta*.
Skilled at wedding embroidery and stitching a bayonet
    wound.
Smoothly chanting Orthodox hymns, whistling *Verkhovyno*,
    or wailing *Dakah Brakha*.

Here is true power, ancient, venerable, established in the

sempiternity of the archetype of the feminine in its four-fold aspect

of mother-hetaera-Amazon-prophetess (de Castillejo, 1985).

Men may run the government, but
Everyone knows Ukrainian women have always had the
    real power.

Since their grandmothers'-grandmothers'-grandmothers'-
grandmother's time
They were all Zaporozhian Cossack brides.

These are gutsy claims in an era that, in a fit of cosmic pique, wishes to ban every binary as merely a patriarchal political artifact, to be overthrown, "deconstructed," in favor of a brave new world of political correctness, as if certain universal laws could be voted away with a petulant "nay" by irate 20-sometings in a privileged cultural legislature. But facts are stubborn things, and metaphysicians as ancient as Lao Tsu and Aristotle and physicists as recent as Bohm and Pauli assure us that if there is one "Big 'T'" truth in the universe it is that the cosmos operates off oppositions—theses and antitheses, in Hegel's terms—that are constantly resolving themselves in the form of syntheses that will themselves in due course become the new theses that kickstart a whole new dialectical process. The Transcendent Function, in brief.

Despite holding a master's degree from the University of Chicago's prestigious School of Social Work, Jankowski is also the son of lower-middle class steel workers from Flint, Michigan, where common sense still holds sway, and where the overly-precious idea of a non-binary universe simply does not pass the sniff-test.

Even more, as a Polish-American who has studied history deeply, especially Eastern European history, Jankowski, who feels his Slavic heritage mightily, knows (as indeed philosophers from Heraclitus to Hegel have known) that conflict is woven into every layer of the tapestry of existence on the looms where human fate is spun. However fungible those binaries may prove to be, trying to wish conflict away is a violation of the laws of opposition about how human effort is generated, marshaled, and deployed.

And thus in a poem in this volume entitled "Si Vas Pacem, Para Bellum" (*If you want peace, prepare for war*), Jankowski, never more Slavic than here, observes with irony as pungent as a very dry wine made in a Polish monastery:

> We do not consult Buddha, but gladly invite Sun Tzu,
>   Sobieski and Pilsudski to council.
> Our motto: Better marksmanship *through* mindfulness.
> While others are navel gazing, our diplomats gaze across
>   the Black Sea.
> Let meditators wander in the cloudy tantric. We localize the
>   laser-focus tactic.

Jankowski locates the truth in paradox and casts about looking for a place to park it. That place is, of course, the poem itself, and writing about the paradox is the way he deals with it.

Jankowski, the Hermeneutics of Suspicion and the Hermeneutics of Hope

How are we to look at things? Is the glass half empty or half full? Who is to decide which is which? We are at an impasse. We could vote on it. That's a practical solution but it doesn't change the *actual* status of the water in the glass, which, to return to the initial dilemma, is precisely what people cannot decide on.

The area of philosophy that deals with this question of how to interpret something is called hermeneutics, which actually began in the 19th century in religious studies in order to establish rules for how to interpret sacred scriptures. But today it has generally come to mean the study of how we interpret *any* thing, event, person, or idea. Mind you, hermeneutics is not primarily concerned with *what* conclusions discussants come to. That is their business. Rather, it studies how people come to a conclusion in the first place. What are the rules of interpretation? What rhetorical forms and organization of evidence are considered compelling and valid? Which are seen as misguided, wrong, or even dangerous. And for that matter, what is even considered "evidence" and what simply irrelevant?

In the 19th and 20th-century, the great hermeneutic debate that raged then and that still does is the one between a "hermeneutics of suspicion" (Ricoeur, 1970) and a "hermeneutics of hope" (Homans, 1975) and together they present themselves as yet another seemingly impossible contradiction that Jankowski sets out to face with intrepidity and resolve with charity. So what are these two hermeneutics and how does Jankowski set out to reconcile them in this pageant of paradoxes that *is* his poetry?

Freud is a good example of a hermeneutics of suspicion. He looked at a patient's problems and asked "What is wrong here? How can I contain this psychological illness that has infected my patient, knowing full well that there is only so much I can do in such a brutal world as this and the human being being what he is—a conflicted, confused, needy and greedy animal that can barely contain its surging sexuality and bristling aggressiveness and is all too ready to use main force if necessary to get what it wants." On the other hand is the "hermeneutics of hope," exemplified by Jung. He looked at a patient's situation and asked, "What is right here? How is nature—which is essentially good and purposeful—offering help to the patient to carve out an even and ever better existence for herself?

What is the higher vision embedded in the illness, and where is the *imago Dei,* the image of God, at the center of my patient's psychospiritual dynamics, for therein lies the cure."

By this point, it should not surprise the reader that Jankowski—as a therapist, cultural critic and poet—deploys the transcendent function to resolve this hermeneutic dilemma. In response to the question, "Should we despair or hope at our present situation historically, politically, and ethically?", Jankowski's answer is "Yes!"

There is certainly occasion for despair in this volume. It is, after all, set against the backdrop of a patently unjust war waged by a superpower under the guidance of an imperialistic, totalitarian bully wreaking havoc on a heretofore peaceful and relatively defenseless state. Russia again, the scourge of the latter half of the 20th century. Russia, which President Reagan called, not without some justification, "the axis of evil in the modern world" (although he was roundly derided for calling a spade a spade, while hundreds of millions under crushing, eviscerating Soviet rule at the time probably secretly cheered that he had done so—when, that is, they could be certain there was no KGB agent within earshot for at least a few minutes). Russia, now under the failing control of a former KGB agent, whose craven antics, both personally and politically, would make even other dictators blush.

As a Pole with a long and acute historical memory, Jankowski is wrenchingly aware of what this all means in Ukraine today. Indeed, he wrote this volume in solidarity with that country and its people.

> Since the conception of this book and the second
>   phase of the war (both beginning on my
>   birthday),
> I have corresponded with Ukrainians clandestinely
> And written these poems for them.

It is not a new story, these killing fields that Russia has carved out of rotting flesh and diabolically moistened with human blood. In "A Polonia Speaks to Ukrainians about Betrayal," Jankowski recounts the nightmarish litany of sorrows and horrors that the Great Bear has visited on the heads of all Slavic people.

> Deportation, starvation,
> Siberia, Katyn Irpin Bucha,
> The mutual massacre at Volhynia.[1]
> Molotov-Ribbentrop, roundup,[2]
> Mass murder cover-up.
> Renunciation, relocation, humiliation,
> Steppe to steppe,
> A trail of sorrows to Uzbekistan.[3]

And thus, in "The Wastelands Tyrants Create," Jankowski, in full throat, intones a threnody, sings his solidarity with the suffering of not only Ukraine but of every nation that has felt the cruel oppressor's rod and suffered the consequences, especially the nauseating consequences of war on a nation's children:

> What for the fleeing child, just outside a refugee center's
>   safe glow?
> Soon to be trafficked by pimps
> Posing as distant relatives of the naïve and terrified youth.
> Now the child is bound for Amsterdam, L.A., Rio, Moscow,
>   Delhi, Dubai, Johannesburg,
> And other Michelin-featured venues.

> Tonight, whether religious or not, everyone hears the cry of
>   desolation from the Cross.
> Everyone clutches invisible prayer beads or rosaries,
> Everyone silently screaming, like Munch's man on the
>   bridge.

What can assuage, what can even begin to contain the magnitude of this misery? Yet, it is in precisely the moment that we ask this question out of the morass of our despair, that from the fullness of our hearts, the answer comes to us—or at least it comes to Jankowski—in the form of the Divine Feminine. It is She who sees all, nurtures all, and helps all, and She never fails us. For Jankowski, the apotheosis of the Divine Mother archetype is in Mary, Our Lady, the Mother of God, the *Theotokos,* as he is fond of addressing her in both his private devotions and his public poetry. For some, and perhaps even many, of the readers of the poetry of Kyle Jankowski, this particular manifestation of the Feminine Face of God may not lie within their spiritual repertoire. But as Jankowski the Jungian would probably hasten to remind us at this concluding juncture, the archetype of the Salvific Feminine is available to all of us, and it is possible to access it, to access *Her,* through our own devotions, after our own manner, as the final Transcendent Function, in Whom all conflicts come to their satisfactory, even felicitous conclusion. One cannot help but think of Dante's final vision of Mary as the Eternal Rose at the end of *The Divine Comedy.*

In this hard-hitting, controversial book of quite singular poetry, Jankowski, one of the most notable young poets of his generation, shows us, indeed models for us out of the depth of his own suffering, how we may all find that cosmic zone of teleological confidence where the impossible, otherwise unweatherable tempest of human suffering finds unbroken safe haven and unending calm in the deathless Port of her Eternal Embrace—Our Lady of Perpetual Help, as Jankowski addresses her in the dedication, as the Great Mother as others might choose to picture and petition Her, but, in any case, as Jankowski concludes, in

> Her
> Light
> Heaven
> Mary
>
> The Lady
> Divine Mother
>
> Our Lady of the Woods
>
> The Lady of Czestochowa
>
> The *Theotokos*
> *Matka Boza*
>
> Maryja
> Garden
> Dark
> She

In the soft effulgence and fructifying presence of the Feminine Divine, Jankowski, in poetic acts that suffer the paradoxes of desolation, finds, also in the poetic act in service of the Feminine Aspect of the Divine, not only rebirth for Ukraine but resurrection for himself, restoration for the reader, and, finally, reconstitution for all the world.

Now, Spring in Ukraine—

Breaking through a long winter's cold, the war.

After a day's work, a family sits on the crocus-lined bank of
the glass-smooth Dnipro.

The spring wheat already climbing toward the azure sky,
today unhazed by artillery smoke.

They pray, with silent gratitude, to that which cultivates
life—

God,

The God-bearer,

Mother Ukraine.

References

Castillejo, I. (1985). *Knowing Woman.* Sigo Press.
Homans, P. (1975). *Jung in Context: Modernity and the Making of a Psychology.*
University of Chicago Press.
Miller. J. (2004). *The Transcendent Function: Jung's Model of Psychological Growth Through
Dialogue with the Unconscious.* State University of New York Press.
Ricoeur, P. (1970). *Freud and Philosophy: An Essay on Interpretation.* Yale University
Press.

INTRODUCTION

The Russian War in Ukraine began on my birthday, twice (2014 and 2022). Having been raised among many Ukrainians in Flint, Michigan, and as a historically informed Polonia, I immediately understood what kind of war this was. As a thoroughly self-read student of WWII and the Holocaust (Jewish and Polish), I remain keenly, painfully aware of where this war is going, and what will be dug out of the ruins after armistice is signed.

This war is as much a major modern propaganda campaign (largely conducted through social media) as it is comprised of traditional maneuvers. Fake news and misinformation are often as deadly as the bullets. I felt immediately morally compelled to volunteer my skills. Though not personally affiliated with the NAFO/OFAN internet counter propaganda organization, I count these "Fellas" as allies in this information war of attrition, with a similar mission. Ukraine has millions (perhaps billions) of civilian allies conducting "psy-ops" in the place official counterespionage and counter propaganda wings of government and military find hardest to reach, the family table. Each working to intelligently satirize the absurd ahistorical and amoral distortions that have savage consequences for real peoples' lives, inside and outside Ukraine.

From February 24, 2022 to Summer 2023, I dedicated every evening (after attending to my own therapy patients and clinic duties) researching, writing and editing this collection. *Dispatches from the Dnipro* is a celebration of the triumph of the human spirit and resistance of freedom loving people while amidst great suffering, apocalypse, and some of the worse things we know human beings are capable of, especially during war. My father's father worked in the war factories in Flint (WWII). My mother's grandfather returned from WWII (CBI Theater) with unaddressed PTSD. His brother died liberating Europe. His wife's brother, Joe, also died fighting in that war. Neither of my grandfathers ever seemed to have words to tell their war stories adequately. I do not feel this poetry collection is bound by the borders of Ukraine, and I hope that many veterans across the generations can see their own stories in these pages. Perhaps it can bring them some meaning, sadness, pride, closure.

As Norman Davies (lauded scholar of European and Polish History) recently said of the War in Ukraine, "what people learn of [Eastern European] history is often the Russian version of history". Dear reader, as this war drags on, and later in the inevitable rebuilding, listen, learn, discern. Also remember, what Leon Trotsky, a leader in the Russian Revolution said, "you may not be interested in this war, but this war is interested in you." As you read *Dispatches from the Dnipro,* no matter your traditions, remember and contemplate the historical events of Fatima, Portugal 1917—"pray for the Heart of Russia". Pray for *all* those harmed by this war. Pray for its end. Do real impactful work for the refugees of this war and wars that will follow. Use your mind to see-through authoritarianism's false comforts and true costs. Remember, when you use your right to vote, organize, speak and teach your children.

Slava Ukraini! Heroiam Slava!

Kyle Jankowski, November 2023

———

WAR LETTERS

"The main task is to pull Ukrainian history out of the Russian shadow. It has to be shown that Ukraine's past has many more contexts than the Russian one—Greek, Roman, Medieval Europe, Renaissance Europe, Polish-Lithuanian Commonwealth, The Reformation, Holy Roman Empire/ Hapsburg Monarchy, Jewish culture, Muslim Crimean Tartars...the Russian context looks like one among many, and not even the main one."

– Yaroslav Hrytsak [1]

Reference
1. Palikot, Aleksander. "Interview: a War of Independence: Six Months into Russia's Invasion, a Ukrainian Historian Takes Stock". Radio Free Europe/Radio Liberty. 23 August, 2022. https://www.rferl.org/a/ukraine-war-six-months-hrytsak-interview/32001079.html

War Letters

"The loss of memory by a nation is also a loss of its conscience." - Zbigniew Herbert[1]

Since the conception of this book and the second phase of the war
       (both beginning on my birthday),
I have corresponded with Ukrainians clandestinely
And written these poems for them.

One moves among Kyiv's dark basements
       (documenting destruction), another
Is trapped in occupied Kherson
       (filling canvasses with disappearing national icons, coloring
       each with her tears), another
For now lives in nervous-peace, around the *mostly* untouched
countryside
       (photographing Ukraine's oldest resource, the land).
Every day, all of us equally expect victory tragedy life and death.
As the Polish proverb goes: "She who cries during life, dies
       smiling."
Even with compulsory post-Soviet English lessons, some of our best
       exchanges are
Lost in translation. We all dread
The ongoing westward march of "avant-garde" Moscow politics.

The Ukrainians' every letter echoes that old Polish Proverb, "Hope
       is the mother of the stupid."

But it's not all cynicism and futility.

My Ukrainian sisters and brothers,
Remember what your Polish cousins said during *Solidarność* and
       Martial Law,[2]
"Shame borne patiently."

Slava Ukraini!

What the Firebird Knew
(Good Friday, 2022)

The Earth will be made clean from the enemies of God—and the Tzar! [1]

This epic is pan-Slavic, but the story belongs to us all. The soul rising up to fight a dark magician, the one who demands outrageous things and clouds the people's minds.

Tonight, the stage and The Chicago Symphony Orchestra are flanked by the Gold and Azure of the Ukrainian flag and the American Stars and Stripes. Performing the Russian epic, Stravinsky's *Firebird Suite*,[2] the performance is a *mélange* of international skills.

Stravinsky lived through three historical epochs, from the days when Cossacks perched on Russian Dons rocketed across the Crimean Peninsula, to Soyuz rockets flying from Kazakhstan toward the cosmos.

Stravinsky knew the dark Russian soul, telling the ancient cautionary tale in a new assonance that is a higher harmony with its strains of fiddles and cellos flying through the fog of war. Lady Virtue makes tyrants tumble from their towers. [3]

The firebird's spirit still protects us.

1. From the opening to "The Firebird" on which Igor Stravinsky ballet.
2. "The Firebird" From *Old Peter's Russian Tales*, Arthur Ransome (1916).
3. *Mr. Cogito* (Polish: *Pan Cogito*). 1974. Polish poet, Zbigniew Herbert.

The Enemy is Us
(For Victor, a Ukrainian journalist)

The true enemy is us,
Jaded, burned out, or beaten into submission,
Seduced by a war chant
Night after night from the electronic prophets,
Talking heads, quick chat boards,
And the cheap entertainment of specious newscasts.

I hear the spectral lament of our ancestors,
The disappeared in Moscow, Mariupol, Buenos Aires, Bogota,
      Kigali, Wounded Knee, Phnom Penh, Katyn.
In any language it sounds the same.

They will not go quietly into that dark night.

The enemy is the humiliation of our broken dreams broken backs
      and broken spirits,
Or just plain old being broke.

The enemy is the people who squandered their inheritance.

The enemy is our covenant with power messiahs,
Propped up by lackies and amateur stock market hustlers,
Some of whom find their way into presidential cabinet meetings as
      "expert" advisors.

The enemy is succumbing to despots wallowing in the
      exorbitantsties
Of fools'-gold-gilded castles,
Filling our heads with only grim fairy tales.
Distraught, we quake at even merely mental paper tigers.

How to stop terrorism, totalitarianism, tyranny?
Repair the schism,
Between your mind and the Divine heart.
Either that or else sink
Into multigenerational alcoholism in forgotten towns and villages.

My Palindrome Birthday
(2/24/22)

My palindrome birthday.
When Truth is spun backwards, lies rush to the phalanx's front.

As the television drones
Around the world,
Children and old people cheer or bemoan
The return of Russia

While we stand mesmerized
With the welfare of street queens, tiger kings, endless-summer
       midlife dreamers,
And prosecuting decades-dead craven priests,
Rather than the tightening chokehold of mad kings
And our things
And rejuvenated war machines

Material Advantage [1]
(For the Ukrainian Armed Forces)

The action isn't in Atlantic City, Las Vegas, Monaco, or Macau.
Who will back David's unevenly-pitched battle against Goliath?
Will you wager on the Ukrainian spirit to endeavor all the way to
their border's finish line? Would you rather stand with the
underdog, one that has refused to tap-out, or gamble with a
predictably cheating Ivan, who frequently is a sore loser? Don't be
fooled by Ivan's overplayed strategy, mostly Aleppo Gambits and
sacrificing all the pawns early on.[2] He still has no material
advantage. Who will bracket an independent Ukraine all the way
through the trials of this March madness? I gladly donate my chips
to the steadfast king in castle Kyiv.

1. As in chess, a material advantage is given to the player who has
   stronger and more numerous pieces remaining on the board.
2. The Aleppo Gambit, an old form of the Queen's Gambit. Conversely,
   the Bishop's Gambit involves the likely sacrifice of the Bishop to set up
   advantageous positions which hopefully will later threaten the
   opponent's high value pieces, mostly the Queen or King.

Homeland

"History is a nightmare from which I am trying to awake." Stephen Dedalus in
Portrait of the Artist as a Young Man

Millions longing for homeland,
Living in a place their fathers and mothers stole.

What kind of inheritance is this?

How do you root
In history's bogs?

VITA, DULCEDO,
ET SPES NOSTRA, SALVE
(OUR LIFE, OUR SWEETNESS,
AND OUR HOPE, SAVE US)

"The sneering disdain that so many secular intellectuals express for religion is a stupidity that has crippled the imagination of our aspiring young artists everywhere."

– Camille Paglia

Nesting Doll Psychology
(For the children of the Soviet Generation now in power)

Bewildered children,
nested inside
Cagey families,
nested inside
Shoddy communities,
nested inside
Untrustworthy governments,
nested inside
A chaotic generation,
nested inside
A fallen world,
nested inside
A decaying godless galaxy,
nested inside
The Divine Heart.

Theotokos [1]

At each revealing, the icon divulges
1,000 words, spoken in complete silence.

Of all the students driven to spread the teachings,

Only one painted.
Clearly the introvert of the bunch.

* * *

Theotokos,
The royal bridge between Western and Eastern Hemispheres
Of our divine mind.

Theotokos,
My soul's will speaks from the dark.
Here I find inspiration again.

Theotokos,
Thy will be done through our will. [2]
It is in our hands.

Theotokos,
Where is the divine child?
My joy has hidden.

Theotokos,
Virgin, before during and after your wounding.
Kore, help me find Sovereignty again.

Theotokos,
Maria Rozwiązująca Węzły. [3]
Please liberate me from the Gordian Knot that has become my life.

Theotokos,
Your Son said turn the other cheek when they strike you,
But you have had enough for one cheek.

—

You make them see:
They *do* know what they do.

1. *Theotokos* (Greek: "Mother of God"). St. Thomas associated the Arabic icon of *Theotokos* with Mary. Saint Cyril of Alexandria (376-444) argued for the theology of Mary as *Theotokos* ("God bearer") over the compromised understanding *Christotokos* ("Mother of Christ") splitting Christ's two natures. The central question that remains alive today both in Christology and Mariology—was Jesus human, Divine or both?
2. In Classical Mythology, "Thy will, our will" is reference to the direction of Isis' hands (up) vs. Black Madonna's hands (down or holding Christ). This is similar to the prayer of St. Francis of Asisi: "Make me a Channel of Your Peace".
3. *Maria Rozwiązująca Węzły* (Polish: "Mary Untier of Knots"). In Archetypal and Jungian Psychology, and the Greek ontological tradition, "soul" and "psyche" are closely related.

Eikon

Her
Light
Heaven
Mary

The Lady
Divine Mother

Our Lady of the Woods

The Lady of Czestochowa

The *Theotokos*
Matka Boza

Maryja
Garden
Dark
She

Straightening Tool
(For one of my patients)

One howling night,
When even the solid old oaks in the back yard
Were twisting in the thundering commotion overtaking the
countryside,

The Lady of the Wood told me,
Dear one,
Do not make yourself a straightening device for other's crookedness.

There is no unrevealed secret,
Making it all fit together
Like a Japanese puzzle box.

Their home's architecture has no blueprints.
You
Against their fervently trapezoidal way,

Their interior is like an Escher staircase;
No matter the angle of your approach,
In their world, you remain upside down and backwards.

How do we frame out a protected threshold,
To buttress against
Their wailing, whirling gale?

Ink on the Wind

"Seeing his mother and the disciple whom he loved standing near her, Jesus said to his mother, 'Woman, this is your son.' Then to the disciple he said, 'This is your mother.' And from that hour the disciple took her into his home." (John 19:26-27 – NJV)

Each night after a full day's work as a psychotherapist,
Fending off the sting and tedium of the thousand paper cuts that
        the fashionably neurotic
American
Inflicts upon himself and me from
Both their self-inflicted cuts
Inflicts upon himself and me from
(One-thousand concentrated cuts along the artery of my throat)
With the Dollar Store paper of their "dysfunctions"—
As if the soul were just a faulty machine to recalibrate
To official specs

Or of refusing to be a projection screen for their glib atheism
Or embarrassing reboots of Sixties drug fantasies,
And after exorcising the screaming wraiths and that come
Streaming out of their existential quagmires,
And my compulsory reading of the news' alternate "realities,"

I finally return home,
Landing at my campaign desk.

The votive lit,
A chaplet counted,
I sit in silence.

I wait for the ink on the wind
To fill the well in my heart,
Into which I dip the only sword I can wield,

I listen.

For Her tears.

Ink on the wind.

Thinking About Journalism in Russia

Many of us inside and outside Russia are beginning to grasp,
We are beginning to fathom

Why there is nothing else to do.

We are beginning to take to heart the instructions:
Pray the Rosary for the conversion of Russia.

War Marriages

Ukrainian women, the bravest anytime, anywhere!

Especially those who wed volunteers, career soldiers or Red Cross
     medics, who,
Just returned from the front, have mostly been mutilated, tortured,
     even unmanned by a landmine—
Each remains an undaunted, unshakable bride
Of the silent walking wounded.

They know
They will never have a Disney or Hollywood marriage.

Yet, back in Kyiv,
Together at the altar,
They gaze at the icon of Kazan.
Together,
They pray.

A Polish Poet Praises Ukrainian Women

The week before Lent,
In parks, kitchens and community centers,
Both Orthodox and Catholic have gathered together.

The young women of Kyiv are working hard—

Pouring oily diesel into vodka bottles
    (emptied on Fat Tuesday),
Packing grated Styrofoam into those same urns
    (instead of stuffing *Pampushky*)[1]
Rolling their old t-shirts
    (in lieu of *pagac*)[2]
Plunging abandoned cars into dug out barricades
    (instead of rolling *Nalysynky* for Cheesefare Sunday).[3]

The nuns already setup a field hospital in the convent and
    sanctuary
    (no longer just a hospital for sinners).
A rosary hangs on every cot
    (for when the morphine isn't enough).
For the never-to-be-married soldiers, the sisters of mercy will let
    their hair down
    (tearing their habits if necessary, to reveal hopeless
    wounds).

Later this week, the priests will also be busy,
Crossing mothers and grandmothers
With ashes from their dead sons.

Babushka's are still watching over their neighborhoods—

Cleaning church kitchens
    (after cleaning their *Kalashnikov*),
Stitching Easter dresses
    (after repairing rucksacks)
Crating canned meat
    (after loading magazines)
Reminding those born after the curtain fell:

Ukraine has many times prevailed.

1. *Pampushky,* a Ukrainian donut, similar to a Polish *paczki, baked and eaten in pre-Lenten fests.*
2. *Pagac* is a Ukrainian/Slovak flatbread stuffed with potato or cabbage, prepared during fasting/meatless Advent, Lent and Christmas Eve meals.
3. *Nalysynky* Ukrainian-style crepes. Cheesefare Sunday or "Forgiveness Sunday", an Christian Eastern Orthodox pre-Lent (Great Lent) holiday, and last day observant Orthodox Christians eat cheese products until Easter.

COSSACKS AND POLACKS

"One of the problems in the Ukrainian crisis is that very few Westerners know their history, or if they know it, what they learn is what we call the Russian version of history."

– Norman Davies

A Polonia Speaks to Ukrainians About Betrayal[1]
(in honor of Lina Kostenko)

Ukrainian brothers and sisters,
Through the centuries, we Poles have been betrayed.
And like you (let's face it)
We have betrayed each other.
We too have been a people without a country.
We both have witnessed the Vistula and Dnipro run red,
Almost before the ink dried on those sensible Geneva accords.

Our betrayals have had many faces—
      Deportation, starvation,
      Siberia, Katyn Irpin Bucha,
      The mutual massacre at Volhynia.[2]
      Molotov-Ribbentrop, roundup,[3]
      Mass murder cover-up.
      Renunciation, relocation, humiliation,
      Steppe to steppe,
      A trail of sorrows to Uzbekistan.[4]

As you walk through the inferno of Mariupol and Bucha,
Remember:
Witold Pilecki's Auschwitz reports were not initially believed
    either.[5]

1. Polonia, a member of the Polish cultural diaspora, or descendants, affected by various wars, genocide, or dismantlement of the Polish nation (i.e. Partitions of Poland, various uprisings, Polish-Soviet War, World War II, Cold-War).
2. (Ukrainian: Волинська трагедія, "Volyn Tragedy", Polish: Wołyn Tragedy).
3. Molotov-Ribbentrop Pact between Soviet Russia and Nazi Germany, secretly planned to conquer and destroy Poland and its culture through genocide upon or simply enslavement of the Polish population.
4. The Russian forced deportation and genocide of the Crimean Tartars (1700s-Second World War).
5. Witold Pilecki was a Polish Special Forces volunteer who volunteered to be arrested by Nazi occupation authorities, so he could infiltrate the Auschwitz SS Concentration Camp. For two and one-half years inside the death camp, Capt. Pilecki gathered intelligence about the true nature of, plans for, and normal operations of the camp. Eventually, he assisted several prisoners in escaping with him. His 1943 report was mostly ignored by Allied intelligence, the truthful and horrifying details deemed to incredible to be accurate. History has unquestionably proven otherwise. Later, Pilecki fought in the Warsaw Uprising. After the war, Capt. Pilecki was captured by the Communists tortured, show-trialed, and executed for spying against the Communist/ Russian occupation regime of post-war Poland. His report was suppressed by Communist State censors for decades and only recently published in English.

Half Blind

"Grant compassion on the suffering animals, the herd of which is being afflicted by the sickle of death...in Your mercy, take away their suffering and pain." [1]

Who cares for the Creator's creatures
As Mokoš's barley fields burn? [2]
Another senseless destruction, cruelly planned for five years. [3]

Everyone here standing at a crossroads,

Remembering Saint Francis of Assisi's caution—
> *If you have people who will exclude any of God's creatures from the*
> *shelter of compassion and pity,*
> *You will have people who will deal likewise with their fellow humans.*

After a long dark night, hearing Saint Modesto's whispering in
     their dreams,
A young family excavates all the rusting tools
Buried in the ground a generation ago.

They stand before history's forge
     aflame with their fury.
Into the crucible, they release false choices,
     serf or collaborator.
The impurities are hammered out of a rusted red star
     now reformed into true community.
The sickle is straightened and smoothed into a flagpole
     so the homeless can waypoint by the azure and gold.
Even the old hammer, sacrificed,
     is cast into bowls.

This sanctuary makes no class distinction,
Sheltering strays, street dogs, mutts and pure-breed alike.
No creature is euthanized for being half-blind.
     (Before the Divine, we are all half-blind).

1. From the prayer of Saint Modestos Bishop of Jerusalem, written by Saint Nikodemos the Hagiorite.
2. (Ukrainian: Мо́кошь) is a Slavic goddess discussed in the Russian Primary Chronicle ("Tales of Bygone Years" by Nestor and others) written in the Kyivan Rus' (850-1100 C.E.). Mokoš is considered a protector of women's work, animals, women in childbirth. She is the only female deity formed as an idol statue in the Kyiv sanctuary of Vladimir the Great. After the Christian conversion of Ukraine and Russia, Mokoš powers came under the authority of the Virgin Mary and Saint Paraskevia.
3. Ukrainian Holodomor/Terror-Famine (Голодомо́р) 1932-1933, and Soviet 5-Year Plans.

"For Your Freedom and Ours"
(Casimir Pulaski Day, March 2022, U.S.A.)

A mix of mostly elderly Poles, Ukrainians, Italians, and Filipinos
Gather silently in the chapel, waiting for our Sister to begin the
Rosary.

I glance sidelong at the icon of Our Lady of Czestochowa.
Her eyes, mirroring our sorrow, also summon our hope.

Her countenance reminds us, as it did Lech Wałęsa, how
Without vigilance and action, freedom is wantonly slain.

In the stilled chapel, I hear
Pulski's rallying cry:

"For your freedom and ours!"

Growing Freedom
(In honor of Ukrainian parents)

In Ukraine,
Mothers and fathers still remember they are the future's caretakers.
Each day, after dressing and feeding the children, they then
      dedicate themselves to their lifelong work:
Resurrecting a starved, exiled and slaughtered culture
      (the soul of the nation).

In this way, they are more animating than any Berkeley feminist.

Deftly, they embroider contemporary *vyshyvka* on new Levi's and
      rustic wedding vests.
With untethered tongues, they tell the story of their almost
      forgotten ancestry.
With hands ever ancient ever new, they spin out the links and
      mend the tears, on the tapestry of Ukraine's cultural loom.

In this way, they are more avant-garde than the latte-laden scene
      in California and New York.

And though he reminded so many of the old Polish *Szlachta* elite,
Tymko Padura remains welcome wherever the people's poetry and
      storied-songs come together. [1]

In this way, they are more sophisticated than "artists" in The
Village, Chicago or Santa Fe.

Studying Taras Shevchenko's verse
Rather than memorizing American hip hop lyrics, vulgar and
      terse.
Whole families spinning *Hopak* in lieu of twerk or modern
      spasmodic lurch.

In this way, they cultivate freedom more than trotting-out traumas
      of serfdom.

And even though Czesław Miłosz, the great anti-Communist,
      defected to American comforts,
No one in modern Ukraine is envious.
Everyone here knows Southern California doesn't hold a torch to

Odessa's beaches or Sevastopol's summers.

Today in the besieged cities, modern Ukrainian parents remember
what was said during Poland's *Solidarnośći* [2]

"The people will give strength to their poet."

And the poet will give strength to the people.

1. Tymko Padura (Polish: "Tomasz Padura"), a 19th Century Polish-
   Ukrainian Romantic poet. Padura's father participated in the
   Kosciuszko Uprising against the Russians and the Partition of Poland.
   Tymko wrote in Ukrainian language, and was a traveling bard, singing
   folk songs promoting Ukrainian and Cossack independence.
2. In 1981, at the Gdansk Shipyards, members of the *Solidarność* (Polish:
   "Solidarity" Movement) honored Czeslaw Milosz with a banner. It
   referenced the memorial for workers that had been killed ten years
   prior in a riot, as the free (non-communist) trade union formed. On the
   memorial was a passage from the Book of Psalms, previously translated
   by Milosz into Polish: "The Lord will give strength unto his people.

Slavic Brethren
(Poland, Spring 2022)
"They broke bread in their homes and ate together with glad and sincere hearts."
(Acts 2:46 - NIV)

Mary of Czestochowa,
You inspire us to reveal our scars.
They embolden our resolve.
Reminding us, in times like these,
So much else becomes trivial.

Many Poles decided to set aside age-old grievances with Hetman
Bohdan Khmelnytsky,[1]
And exclaimed in one voice—
> *In the tyranny of war, there is no prejudice in our hearts.*
> *Ukraine, you are our brothers and sisters!*

So they gave the bedraggled women, staggering from the trains,
poppies and lilies.
> To remind them, no matter how cold the war, everything
> blossoms again.
And toys to the quaking children,
> To help hold on to a bit of innocence.
And doctors and nurses eased arthritic old ones to chairs,
> Like each was a king or queen.
And the newsmen and writers and poets stopped talking,
> Instead listened, night after night to the people's stories.
Homes opened, with that familiar Polish hospitality.

Even the Trumpeter of Krakow has changed his tune.
The *Hejnal* bugle's warning, already too late.
The enemy is at the gates of Kyiv.
Shche ne vmerla Ukrainy! rings from the Wawel Castle ramparts,[2]
Echoing Kosciuszko's voice from another dire age,
Poland is not yet lost.[3]

1. The Zaporozhian Cossack leader, Khmelnytsky, led The Great Revolt (1648) against the Polish nobles (*szlachta*) and the Polish-Lituanian Commonwealth, helping further Ukrainian independence. Simultaneously, the rebellion significantly contributed to the end of the Polish Golden Age and downfall of the Commonwealth.
2. *Shche ne vmerla Ukrainy!* (Ukrainian: Ще не вмерла України, "Ukraine has not yet perished"). The national anthem of Ukraine. Based on a poem (1862) by Pavlo Chubynsky and set to music (1863) by Mykhailo Verbytsky, a Greek-Catholic priest.
3. *Poland is Not Yet Lost* (Polish name: *Mazurek Dabrowskiego*) the national anthem of Poland, written by Jozef Wybicki (1797) following the 3rd Partition of Poland, the final dissolving of the Polish nation by the occupation of Prussia, Austria-Hungary, and Russia.

The Falcons are Returning to Ukraine [1]
(Dnipropetrovsk Zaporozhian Cossack-style song for children)

The falcons are returning to Ukraine
From foreign lands near and far,
Hang on, little sparrows, hang on.

On Eagles wings, we're ancestral land bound,
Hang on, little sparrows, hang on.

The falcons are fighting, in metropolis and country town,
Hang on, little sparrows, hang on.

The falcons are taking the rabid bear down,
Hang on, little sparrows, hang on.

Hang on, hang on, little sparrow of mine
As the birches bend with the westward storm.

Hang on, hang on, little sparrow of mine
Soon the terror of war will be no more.

Hang on, little sparrows, hang on.

If we die, let's die together, my lovely sparrow.
Bury our hearts nowhere else but in green Ukraine.

1.   (Ukrainian: "Гей, соколи"), Polish: "Hey, Falcons!"), also known by *Żal za Ukrainą* (*Longing for Ukraine*) and *Na Zielonej Ukrainie* ("In Green Ukraine"). Written by either the Ukrainian-Polish poet Tomasz Padura (1801-1871) or Polish-Slovak music composer, Maciej Kamieński (1734-1821). The song was very popular during the Polish-Soviet War and WWII. This represents my version, a combination of the spirit of many versions and English translations of the original songs. Any errors in translation or cultural misunderstanding are my own.

Si vis pacem, para bellum
"If you want peace, prepare for war."

Thank you, America, but we are one nation under Our Lady.
Molly Pitcher can pour a drink for Irena Sendler, [1]
While Marie Currie schools Francis Crick on ethics.

We prefer The Polish Way.

Franco-Prussian military strategy fares poorly in the East.
(But if it must be Western, let it be Patton, not De Gaulle.
After the bullets and the barricades, Barbara Kostrzewska, not
        Piaf.) [2]
Pass on the yogurt. We prefer dill.
Croissants? We are suspicious of crescents on table or banner.

We do not consult Buddha, but gladly invite Sun Tzu, Sobieski and
        Pilsudski to council. [3]
Our motto: Better marksmanship *through* mindfulness.
While others are navel gazing, our diplomats gaze across the Black
        Sea.
Let meditators wander in the cloudy tantric. We localize the laser-
        focus tactic.

A waning crescent eventually renews itself to fullness.
Even the rusted sickle can be sharpened.
Hammers have but three purposes—blacksmithing, war, and
        rebuilding home after.

Si vis pacem, para bellum.

1. Irena Sendlerowa (Sendler), a Polish Catholic Social Worker, who famously helped smuggle children out of the ghetto and hid them in Catholic Polish homes and convents. Very late in life, for her work, Irena was awarded the distinction Righteous Among Nations (from Israel) and the Order of the White Eagle (Poland's highest civilian award).
2. Barbara Kostrzewska was a famous Polish Singer and theater director who worked for the resistance and participated in the WWII Warsaw Uprising. Edith Piaf of France, a beloved and internationally renowned singer whose controversial biography suspects her being favored by both the Nazis and French *Résistance*.
3. King John III Sobieski led the Holy League's armies to victory against the Ottoman Turks at Vienna (1683, September 11-12). Sobieski led the largest cavalry charge in history. Pilsudski was one of hero generals and strategists of the Polish-Soviet War and served as the first Inter-war Period President of the Polish Republic.

Slav Incognito [1]

Your ancestry is hidden in plain sight.

White people, remember,
Our White Eagle
Flying for over 1,000 years.

It's not Hip-Hop echoing across our lands.
Dressage clip-clop or its flare.
Sarmatia style never goes out of fashion.

Sunflower seeds.
Doesn't everyone's uncle eat those by the handful?

Kielbasa, not "just sausage."
Those baseball park hot dogs?
About as American as Nathan Handwerker's Coney Island
creations.

Birthplace of those famous Bud suds?
Middle Europe, not the Midwest.
Czech your sources.

Polish Rummy? Nah, just cards,
Everyone important knows the rules.

Kowalski's?
"A typical neighborhood bakery."
No one mentions the three-hundred-year-old Galician pastry
recipes.

That's not grandma's boring old bundt pan,
It's Easter *Babka* that your *babica's babcia* wants you to bake again.

In Scouts,
Honor, loyalty and marksmanship
Garner greater praise than knots.

Your ancestry is hidden in plain sight.

1. It is estimated that over ten million of America's "white people" (aka. racially "Caucasian" Americans) are actually of primarily Polish descent. Millions more are of various Slavic ethnicities and intermarriages with fellow Slavs. The popularly and ease of DNA testing will likely increase this number. Galicia is a region of southern Poland near the Carpathian Mountains where the Kowalski Family is believed to originate. Kowalski's bakeries, markets and sausage makers are famous in Polish and other Slavic communities around the American Midwest, especially Minneapolis/St. Paul (Minnesota), Fort Wayne (Indiana), Toledo (Ohio), Hamtramck/Detroit and Grayling (Michigan).

The Blue and the Gold

On this unusually crisp Palm Sunday, I set out into the wilderness.
Tying two bandannas around my greyhound's naked neck, one
      royal blue, one gold,
I think of Ukraine's still cool hued skies and frosted and faded
      flaxen fields.

The blue and the gold were woven into my fate long before my
      birth—
      The Polish *Jastrzębiec* Clan,
            to which I owe half my ancient heraldry.
      The coat of arms of the ancient Jankowski family line,
            one of the first families knighted and bestowed the
            title *Szlachta,* for chivalric service and sacrifice to the
            young burgeoning Polish Kingdom.
    My *alma mater*, The University of Michigan,
            arena gridiron tournaments where sport stands in
            for warfare, the source of this simple blue kerchief
            now adorning my loyal hound.

Later that week, conditioning for the annual Chicago Polish
      Marian Pilgrimage
            (the source of the gold scarf)
I traverse tarnished but reclaimed Midwestern prairies,
Long cold, now thawing, brightening, gradually enlivening,
With Spring songbirds and blooming birches.

Painfully, I envisage my Ukrainian friends living among missile
      cratered golden grain fields.

Here each morning, many young Eastern Europeans calmly jog
      this same path,
While across the ocean, their cousins run from the latest morning
      to evening shelling—
            At a community park, a gymnasium, a shopping
            center, a school, other legitimate targets.

A dictator needs no justification. [1]

1. *Ukase*, an edict of the Russian (historically Tsarist) government. Often an arbitrary command. Edicts often have a meaning implying enmeshed religious/state authority. Or through a psychological lens, the ego-driven or narcissistic will of the authoritarian ruler, a command which, ironically, may be contradictory to their long-term stability as ruler. An excess of edits is often the fertilizer of popular uprisings and revolutions of the lorded-over classes.

Ode to the Daughters of Ukraine

Men may run the government, but
Everyone knows Ukrainian women have always had the real
      power.
Since their grandmothers'-grandmothers'-grandmothers'-
      grandmother's time
They were all Zaporozhian Cossack brides.

Ukrainian *women*—
      Comfortable oiling Kalashnikovs and iron skillets.
      Equally clever with navigating home economics, Soviet
      Five-Year-Plans and selling their elegant paintings through
            internet commerce.
      Adept at scientific matters, I.T. centers, translating Cyrillic
            and Latin letters.
      Unashamedly proficient at soothing children, animals, and
            mental patients.
      Experts in laundry room, boardroom and bedroom.
      Adroitly dancing across battlefields with *Shashka*, or manor
            house with *szlachta*.
      Skilled at wedding embroidery and stitching a bayonet
            wound.
      Smoothly chanting Orthodox hymns, whistling *Verkhovyno*,
            or wailing *Dakah Brakha*.

These passionate women, no matter their age,
Delight in—
Marinating wedding meats, poetry, or philosophy, until the
      perfect moment,
Jumping fires with their mates and children on Ivana
      Kupala,
Painting their nails and *pysanka* for Easter festivities,
Dancing and clowning like gypsies during Malanka,

Remembering always a chair and plate for the unexpected
      Christmas guest.

Tribute to Ukraine's Theater Troupes
(March 2022)

Huddled in bomb shelters, designed and built by people that perfected the theater of politics, troupes from Kyiv huddle with children on their makeshift stages (more Soviet grey than proper black box). The children know the courageous and clever underdog hero Ivasyk-Telesyk of Ukrainian myths and legends, also inspires their parents and grandparents to create the makeshift battlements of Fortress Kyiv. This Spring's project is perhaps more ambitious than anything these troupes have ever produced.

These young critics are still too nervous to clap or boo, as they hear the rockets and shells above. Though the show will be more memorable than the rapid-fire short videos blowing up the internet. More therapeutic for assuaging their fears than a constant drip of apps, dance crazes and pop-culture-sugar their Western peers suck from the IV of the TV. The cynics say such stories are dispensable vestiges of an antique era. But the people need traditional heroes and stories to remember what is real.

ODES TO
THE NEW FIREBIRD

"The Terror-Famine of 1932-33 was a dual-purpose byproduct of collectivization, designed to suppress Ukrainian nationalism and the most important concentration of prosperous peasants at one throw."
– Norman Davies

Graffiti on a Wall of a Collapsed Ukrainian School

Take up our peril, you who know,
We had no quarrel with our present foe.

Brief to an Aspiring Tyrant

First, promote propaganda passing itself off as entertainment. The more one-sided the better. Prey on people's historical fears, unhealed traumas, and grandparents' war stories. Create and fund anti-social media. Remember that xenophobia is your best weapon. Excoriate all contradictory opinions and facts as foreign corruption.

Second, censor local media. Arrest factual journalists and intrepid dissidents. Trick and seduce children into exposing their teachers' and parents' critiques of the state. But also remember, even children cannot be trusted. Make very public examples of those who have failed in their duty to the state. Proclaim all these draconian measures in the interest of national security.

Third, create strawmen, both of everyday citizens and armies. Dehumanize that enemy. Coopt the natural patriotism of youth, their passion to serve their country. Use it to convert them into sub-rosa agents of all sorts in every reach of life. Brand all inherently ethical paradoxes as merely political errors to be reeducated out of—violently if necessary.

Fourth, mandate military conscription, but no other national service. Keep ethical inquiry at a minimum. Build upon earlier indoctrination. Send troops with limited, and spoiled, rations. Encourage pillaging. Justify it as the simple spoils of war. Recruit sociopaths, psychopaths, and other shady characters. Provide them off-record military training and funding. grant enormous autonomy. Give intelligence agencies innocuous names and catchy initials.

Fifth, put together a friendly and sanitized private contractor social-media portal. Insert into conflict zones to "advise" in resolving "ethnic tension." Ban humor: There is nothing funny about the total state.

Sixth, plan a genocide to be carried on under the cover of a righteous war. Label all civilians who do not evacuate as being loathsome partisans. Organize and implement reprisals against ordinary people. Rape and child torture are most effective.

78

Wholesale slaughter is a sloppy last resort. Hold press conferences with international media. Justify your "counter-terrorism mission."

Seventh, respond to foreign criticism by providing pre-packaged "investigative journalism." Threaten families, business partners, and friends to assure compliance.

Eighth, verbosely defend the honor and integrity of your flawless and brave army. Court martial any soldiers who reveal what is really happening in the barracks and on the battlefield. Discredit leaked reports as misinformation or foreign conspiracy. Deny the true number of casualties, soldier and civilian. Offer their families a resort vacation in a far-away place. Assure silence. Move dead civilians into unmarked graves. Force-evacuate civilians into bare-bones, crushed bones "processing centers" to "assure their safety." Bring your own "humanitarian aid" team with asphyxiating strings attached on recipient cultures to secure the hegemony of the donor culture. Block the International Red Cross.

Ninth, hide wounded troops from cameras. Real treatment and rehabilitation optional. For the survivors, send in psychiatrists with "miracle drugs."

Tenth, remind dissidents of their pensions, families' safety, and that non-compliance of any sort is now tantamount to treason. Close the border to the enemy nation. Confiscate humanitarian aid filled with "smuggled weapons." Ban your citizens and remaining journalists from traveling to the war zones. Occupy other enemy's nation with peacekeepers. Rest assured that you have stamped your name on the pages of history.

Begin again at Step 1. Repeat.

Russian Grey

How grotesque the enemy who scorns peace.

A foe who wipes their gory hands with your white flag
After soiling your peace treaty, in lieu of the loo.

An adversary whose M.O. is no mercy,
Whose motto is no parlay.

A nemesis as frigid as icicles on Stalin's statue in midwinter
Moscow,
Holding you under the eternal siege of Russian Grey skies.[1]

Especially beware the enemy who only offers two choices:
The gallows or the Cross.

---

1.   Hex Color code for Grey Russian color #8e9598, RGB(142,149,152).

Modern Warfare
"Put on the full armor of God. (Ephesians 6:11 – NJB)

For those in the besieged cities,
Rationing ammunition, food, hope, not sure which will run out
    first,
It is time to put on the full armor of God.

This war isn't pedantically organized like an SS campaign, with its
    efficient executions.
It isn't face-to-face butchery, like Kigali's killing fields.
There will be no grand final cavalry charge toward tanks, cannons,
    or Turks.
No heroic last stands like Westerplatte, Thermopylae or Shiroyama
    will even be possible on these specious battlefields whose
    landmines are words words words and whose trenches are
    dug in the halls of English departments and Cultural
    Studies.

Yet, it is *not* foolish to pray for a miracle on the Dnipro.[1]

This war takes the gold medal for lunacy at the Devil's Olympics—
    Occupiers with expired rations destroying fresh food
        warehouses,
    Blasting apart historic landmarks, once jewels of the
        occupier's own culture,
    Burning maternity hospitals, schools, and retirement
        homes,
    Destroying—through their rape of a brother-nation's
        narratives
    That nation's *elan* and evolution.

For we wrestle not against flesh and blood,
But against... rulers of the darkness of this world, against spiritual wickedness in
high places. [2]

There are no treaties, surrendering swords, batons or pistols,
No shredded flag lowering while raising another's fresh-pressed
    banner,
No girls kissing young sailors and soldiers on confetti-covered
    streets,

No following marching bands through arches or across memorial
      squares.

There will only be our wounded hearts,
Ripped open as the land.
The eerily silenced apartment blocs, crumbling like the towers of
      our old mutual ideals.

There will only be our wounded hearts,
Sitting quietly in the dark,
By the still smoldering church and library.[3]

1. The Miracle on the Vistula River, Poland, during the Polish-Soviet
   War (August 1920).
2. Ephesians 6:12 – KJV.
3. Psalms 23:4 – KJV.

Koan for The Disappeared

Siberia. A familiar story.
What is the sound
Of one dissident disappearing?

The Wastelands Tyrants Create

On the Feast of Our Lady of Sorrows, I gaze upon the icon,

> *Matka Boża,*[1]
> *Help me quicken to the cries of those who, insane,*
> *Wander through the wastelands tyrants create.*

What for the newlyweds, called to duty on different sides of the
      bloody border?
Both know it's likely a one-way passport in different directions for
      both of them.

What for the old *babusya* of Borodyanka? Childless.
The first choked on Prypyat's dust.
The second gone from grief and *gopnik* drugs.[2]
The third, on the balcony.
Slumped, bound, stiff, his third eye permanently opened
By the horrors of post-modern warfare.

What for the old village widower?
He stands in a blown-out window, staring at his cratered rye fields,
      and oblivion.
As shrapnel and rain pour in upon the family photos
He shakes, mutters, traipses among the caved-in ruins,
The only life he's ever known.

What for the fleeing child, just outside a refugee center's safe
      glow?
Soon to be trafficked by pimps
Posing as distant relatives the naïve and terrified youth.
Now the child is bound for Amsterdam, L.A., Rio, Moscow, Delhi,
Dubai, Johannesburg,
And other Michelin-featured venues.

Tonight, whether religious or not, everyone hears the cry of
      desolation from the Cross.[3]
Everyone clutches invisible prayer beads or rosaries,
Everyone silently screaming, like Munch's man on the bridge.

---

1. *Matka Boża* is a Polish-Catholic title for Our Lady/Mother of God.
2. *Gopnik* is a pan-Slavic language popular term for a gangster, thug, hoodlum.
3. Matthew 27:46

Dispatch from the Dnipro

Tonight the mighty Dnipro roars, not from its rapids but artillery shells and rockets. Quaking animals and people shelter near the great river, an exodus from Kharkiv to Kyiv, Dnipro to Mariupol, Luhansk to Lviv. For now, together their angst bellows with the mighty Dnipro—the main artery that runs through Ukraine—from the hub of Kyiv to the sunflower-filled heartland of Crimea's soothing shores with its warm waves.

Another thundering bellow is heard across the steppe, not far from the river, two armies on the march. Both singing the *Song About the Dnieper River*,[1] both imagine the same enemy, but only one is actually fascist. Bunkered in their homes, the people of Kremenchuk can hear the two armies in counterpoint:

> *Let the blood of the fascist dogs flow like a river,*
> *The enemy will not take our land*
> *Like the spring Dnieper,*
> *All enemies will be swept away*
> *By our army and our people.*

O, Dnipro, the Spring cranes are now flying over you, bringing omens, the birth of two new nations.

Around the campfires, round after round of nostalgia is passed around like outdated issues of *Pravda*. The first army in unison, continues *The Song About the Dnieper River*. Some sing out of fear, some from naivety, some are invincibly ignorant. But the second army with blended peoples of the steppe, begins a new verse together.[2]

---

1. *Song of the Dnieper* (Russian)/*Dnipro* (Ukrainian) *River*, made famous by Soviet-Era Russian bass-baritone singer Leonid Kharitonov, who often sang patriotic songs about the Second World War. The reader is encouraged to listen to the original song at http://www.youtube.com/watch?v=p3aekv1V5RE .
2. *March of the Ukrainian Nationalists*, Oles Babiy (lyrics) and Omelian Nyzhankivskyi (music), originally written in 1929 following the loss of the Ukrainian National Republic (1917-1921) to the Soviet Union and the Second Polish Republic. In 2017, following the loss of Crimea in 2014 to Russia, the song was updated.

Historical Notes on the Russia-Ukraine War
(For the Russian children arrested at the Ukrainian Embassy, Moscow, March 2, 2022) [1]

"Putin is an authoritarian, and, like any autocratic ruler, he thinks that there is not society and public opinion independent of the government. Everything that is called independent is either manipulated or bought." – Yaroslav Hrytsak

It must lance and scar you, split you at history's crossroads
When your leaders spin around the truth
Even more than they rotate their political alliances
Up and down the flagpole. Then

Pagan nomad chiefs become
Orthodox Christian patriarchates become
Feudalists become
Imperialists become
Tzarist white loyalists and black anarchists become
Bolshevist red revolutionaries become

Leftists high on deicide eagerly become
Spy-trained schemers become
Gangster opportunists become
Hyper capitalists become
Oligarch opportunists become
Far-Right Nationalists become
Cults of personality become
Infallible icons

Worshipped by
Farmers becoming
Conscripts becoming
Artillery fodder becoming
Modern warfare veterans becoming

Ashes and blood-rusted tags in mobile crematoria
Draped with flags fluttering in the fallout.

Brave children, may you not languish too-long in your
        grandparents' vicious Siberian cribs,
As history's orphans, yes, but also what we have always been,
        history's custodians.

1. While laying flowers and "no to war" signs at the Ukrainian Embassy in Moscow, Russian children aged 7 to 11 were arrested by Russian police, who then detained and booked the children in jail.

Russian Roulette [1]
(For Boris Romantschenko) [2]

Sin,
A gambling game,
With gambits that craftily claim
To electrify life
But actually deal out the hand of death.

1. "For the wage paid by sin is death..." (Romans 6:23 - NJB).
2. Boris Romantschenko survived internment in *four* WWII German Concentration Camps (Buchenwald, Mittelbau-Dora, Bergen Belsen, Peenemünde). He was killed in his home in Kharkiv, Ukraine, when his apartment bloc was shelled by Russian troops, during Russian President Vladimir Putin's falsely reasoned 2022 "special military operation to de-Nazify Ukraine." Romantschenko served as vice-president of the Buchenwald and Mittelbau-Dora Memorials Foundation, which documents Nazi crimes against humanity and teaches the history of the WWII Holocaust.

Shashlik
(2 Kings 23:10) [1]

And their self-appointed high priest, their KGB messiah,
Rounded up the children in the great square,
Bound them before the iron brasier
Lit with the cannons' unceasing fire.
One after another, sacrificed to the flames,
Skewered like shashlik,
On the thin red line.

Back in Moscow sits old Saturn in Lenin Square,
Eating his children.[2]

1. Molech (Moloch) was a Canaanite Old Testament Biblical god akin to Chronos/Saturn. From Hebrew *melech* ("king"), combined with the vowels of *boshet* ("shame").
2. See Francisco Goya's *Saturn Devouring His Son* for a powerful visual rendering of this.

Russian Soldiers' Wives
(for the wives of Russian soldiers and conscripts sent to Ukraine)

The young wives sitting alone,
Very pregnant or with an infant,
Inside their simple house or apartment,
Waiting for the cold thaw
So they may begin a newlywed's garden.
Optimistic, soon they will share tea with their "war heroes."

The matrons, still youthful
Despite their perpetual scowl,
Widowed since Chernobyl, know:
So many wilt before their prime.

The old babushkas,
Widowed since Afghanistan.
Only their faces, red as borsch,
Betray their boiling anger.

The ancient crones,
Fatherless since the Bolshevists extended "friendship" to Poland
     and Ukraine.
They have seen many governments rise and fall,
As the rye and wheat in their fields.
They teach the younger ones,
Slavic women's strength is like the birch,

While the men are fated to be like giant walnuts,
Constantly put into the jaws of war,
By each era's master conductor or gleeful nutcracker.

Alexandrov and Shostakovich and Tchaikovsky are long dead.

Who will memorialize these things—atrocious and sublime—in the
    latest great symphony?
        Who will compose the next great Russian epic?

Wag the Dog

"For our fight is not against human enemies that we have to struggle, but against the principalities and the ruling forces who are masters of the darkness in this world, the spirits of evil in the heavens." (Ephesians 6:12 - NJB)

Two mothers, neighbors, stand in opposing wings of a Kharkiv funeral home.

The first mourns her only son,
Killed by the other woman's son,
Who was called up for military service, for a war that isn't
     happening,[1]
And shot by his own officers, during strategic withdrawal, that was
     certainly not a rout.

Here, at the end of history, we have finally learned how Satan's
     tale wags the dog.[2]

1.   The role of Stanley Mots (a Hollywood director) played by Dustin Hoffman in *Wag the Dog*, (1997) film directed by Barry Levinson.
2.   When Vladimir Putin's government ordered a mobilization of the Russian armed forces (September 2022), many Russian citizens were shocked, as their journalists and the government have said since February 24, that there is no "war" Ukraine.

—

AFTER
THE GUNS GO SILENT

"Ukraine is a testing ground for the stability of the two competing political models of our era: liberal democracy and authoritarianism. Putin has instrumentalized history as a *casus belli*...'to make Russia great again.' Ukrainians on the other hand, do not want to repeat history, because for them there is too much injustice and suffering there."

– Yaroslav Hrytsak [1]

Reference
1. Palikot, Aleksander. "Interview: a War of Independence: Six Months into Russia's Invasion, a Ukrainian Historian Takes Stock". Radio Free Europe/Radio Liberty. 23 August, 2022. https://www.rferl.org/a/ukraine-war-six-months-hrytsak-interview/32001079.html

After the Guns Go Silent
(For the destroyed Ukrainian churches)

After the guns go silent,
Take these pieces from the old Bloc.
Build a pyre from the shambles of our old lives,

Then sit vigil through the Long Night,
Grieving, as those who intimately witnessed
Ukraine on the Cross.

At sunrise, flames sink to coals.

Marshall your kin toward the crucible
The still-smoldering sanctuary.
Take your finger off the trigger.
Instead, thumb the prayer rope.

Vengeance only pierces Her heart.

Prostrate yourself.
Give the lead to the crucible,
Alms for our new offering bowl.

Stop each other from staring
At coals and ash.
Revision your vocation.
This is the time of rebuilding.

Collect also the shattered colors strewn across the sanctuary.
But do not just melt the shards of the Light together.
They will lose their unique luster.
Instead, bridge them with lead.

Harmony in distinction, yet strongly adjoined,
This is the true paisley path.

In this place that saw Cesar's wanton destruction, rebuild the
temple.

Dear ones,
Do not despair,
The covenant is not broken.

Now, paint our story,
Illuminated with gold.

Resurrection of Ukraine
(For our Slavic cousins)

The kind of faith forged in the same dark nights that make
Madonnas black.
Pressure that makes diamonds from simple stone beads.
History that cycles through decades and eras.

Poland, and her people, on the Cross.

Feast of Assumption 2021,
10,000 Poles and Polonia pray together,
On our knees at the shrine.

Many kneel before Our Lady of Fatima,
Begging for the conversion of the heart of Russia,
We should have prayed harder.

This summer we will again pilgrimage to the shrine.
Together, entering the circle of the Rosary,
Touching the blood-red blossom of Mary's pierced heart.

For the heart of Russia,

And the resurrection of Ukraine.

*Readers may wish to research and view Władysław Barwicki's painting *The Resurrection of Poland*.

In Sunflower Fields

(for the people of Mariupol)

*Set to the melody of the World War 1 memorial poem and song, *In Flanders Fields.*

In Mariupol's fields, gold sunflowers grow,
Sprouting up where children were buried, not long ago,

And with their mothers blooming, in prime of life.
Do not turn your faces away from our strife.

The Spring sparrows sang, their brave hearts' desire,
From under the shattered glass rocks ruin and mire,

The Spirit of Ukraine will never tire!

We are the dead, short days ago
Our hearts felt Ukraine's azure skies glow.

From cowardly lies, we senselessly die.
In war the youth always bleed and waste, on both sides.

Take up our peril with our collective foe!

Can you keep faith, with decency,
Give us justice, not just pity!?

If you break faith, with use who die,
We shall not vanish from God's sight.

Where we fall, golden sunflowers grow tall,
To remind you of us,

Who peacefully lived here,

Near Mariupol's fields.

—

The Easter Sun Rises

The Easter sun rises on Chicago—
Over the near-frozen slough,
Sparkling the still frosted wilted flaxen prairie grasses,
Brightening the ultramarine sky,
Burning the fog off the watery mirror of our hearts.

We stand at the gate of dawn
And we see what it is that we must truly fear:
They who only offers two choices,
The gallows or the cross.

Now, Spring in Ukraine—
Breaking through a long winter's cold, the war.
After a day's work, a family sits on the crocus-lined bank of the
      glass-smooth Dnipro.
The spring wheat already climbing toward the azure sky, today
      unhazed by artillery smoke.

They pray, with silent gratitude, to that which cultivates life—

God,

The God-bearer,

Mother Ukraine.

AUTHOR BIO

Kyle grew up in Flint, Michigan in the 1980s-2000s as the American Auto Industry, economy, schools and local community began to collapse. Born to a large extended Polish/Scottish-American family of auto workers, military veterans, construction workers, nurses and other skilled trades, Kyle witnessed the first-hand suffering of the American Rustbelt de-industrialization, offshoring of jobs, betrayal of labor, urban blight and inevitable class and racial violence. He credits his many mentors and adoptive families for helping him *not* succumb to the fatalism, despair and decay around him.

Despite his extensive training as a clinician and in academia—University of Chicago (AM/MSW), Pacifica Graduate Institute (MA Jungian/Depth Psychology), University of Michigan (BSW), and a 5-year post-graduate advanced clinical training program—it is his Polish and Scottish heritage, his marriage to Vanessa (a brilliant clinician, artist and PhD. scholar in her own right), studies in world religions/philosophy, his Catholic (Universal Church) faith, being an avid lifelong history buff, traveling and the many people that have crossed his path (in clinic and community) that most informs his poetry and other writing. Kyle's clinical work greatly informs his poetry and his desire to keep it relatable and relevant to a wide population.

Outside the clinic, Kyle and Vanessa care for their borderlands property outside Chicago, cultivating and foraging local plants and restoring their small forest plot. Kyle studies Scottish Highland Bagpipes and saxophone, and Vanessa Native American Flute and violin.

READER'S NOTES